LITTLE ME

SID CAESAR
IN
"LITTLE ME"

the new musical comedy

WITH

VIRGINIA MARTIN

AND

NANCY ANDREWS

BOOK BY	MUSIC BY	LYRICS BY
NEIL SIMON	CY COLEMAN	CAROLYN LEIGH

BASED ON A NOVEL BY PATRICK DENNIS

with

MORT MARSHALL	JOEY FAYE	SWEN SWENSON	
NANCY CUSHMAN	PETER TURGEON	MICKEY DEEMS	ADNIA RICE

SCENERY & LIGHTING BY	COSTUMES BY	VOCAL ARRANGEMENTS BY
ROBERT RANDOLPH	ROBERT FLETCHER	CLAY WARNICK

ORCHESTRATIONS BY	DANCE MUSIC ARRANGED BY
RALPH BURNS	FRED WERNER

MUSICAL DIRECTION BY CHARLES SANFORD

Musical Numbers & Dances Staged by BOB FOSSE

Directed by CY FEUER and BOB FOSSE

Paul Bacon

ISBN 978-1-4234-9834-6

HAL•LEONARD® CORPORATION

7777 W. BLUEMOUND RD. P.O. BOX 13819 MILWAUKEE, WI 53213

T0087256

For info on Notable Music Co. Inc./The Cy Coleman Office, visit
www.notablemusic.net or email us at **info@notablemusic.net**

Visit Hal Leonard Online at
www.halleonard.com

CONTENTS

Cy Coleman

Cy Coleman was a musician's composer, classically trained at piano, composition, and orchestration at New York City's High School for the Performing Arts and NY College of Music. Mr. Coleman was being groomed to be the next great conductor. Instead he turned his passion to jazz and formed the popular Cy Coleman Trio. Born Seymour Kaufman on June 14, 1929 in the Bronx, he changed his name at age 16 in time to use it on his first compositions with lyricist Joe A. McCarthy ("Why Try to Change Me Now," and "I'm Gonna Laugh You Right Out of My Life"). While still performing in jazz clubs and enjoying a successful recording career, Cy began writing with veteran songwriter Carolyn Leigh. Hits like "Witchcraft" and "The Best Is Yet to Come" were followed by their leap to Broadway with *Wildcat*, starring Lucille Ball ("Hey, Look Me Over") and then *Little Me* ("I've Got Your Number" and "Real Live Girl"). In 1966 Cy, along with legendary lyricist Dorothy Fields, triumphed with the smash hit *Sweet Charity* ("Big Spender," "If My Friends Could See Me Now"). Cy continued on Broadway and wrote the scores for *Seesaw, I Love My Wife, On the Twentieth Century, Barnum, City of Angels, The Will Rogers Follies,* and *The Life.* In 2004 Cy returned to his roots and revived the Cy Coleman Trio, once again wowing the audiences with his amazing skill at the piano. In Mr. Coleman's amazing career he took home three Tony® Awards, two GRAMMY Awards®, three Emmy® Awards, an Academy Award® nomination, and countless honors. Cy served on the Board of ASCAP for three decades.

DEEP DOWN INSIDE

Music by CY COLEMAN
Lyrics by CAROLYN LEIGH

Moderately bright Hoe-down tempo

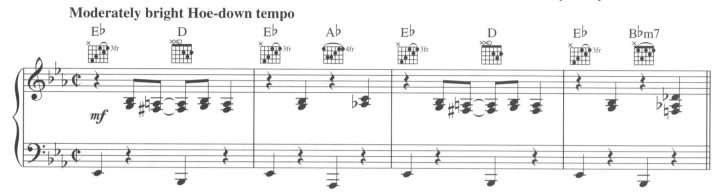

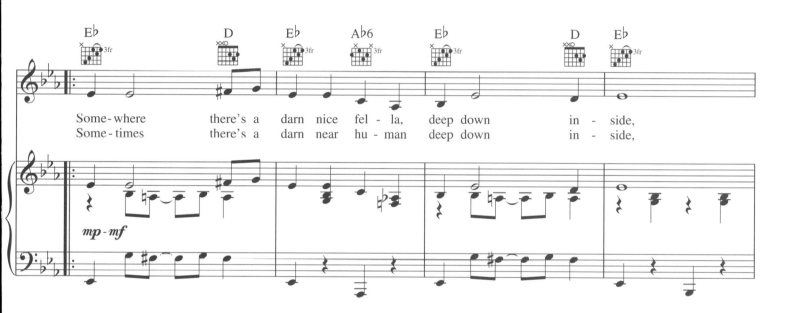

Some-where   there's a   darn   nice   fel - la,   deep   down   in - side,
Some-times   there's a   darn   near   hu - man   deep   down   in - side,

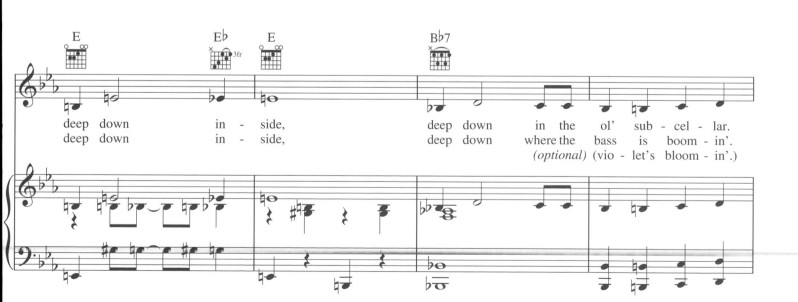

deep   down   in - side,   deep   down   in   the   ol'   sub - cel - lar.
deep   down   in - side,   deep   down   where   the   bass   is   boom - in'.
(optional) (vio - let's   bloom - in'.)

TO BE A PERFORMER

Music by CY COLEMAN
Lyrics by CAROLYN LEIGH

Moderato

Are you a ma-gi-cian? A tal-ent-ed bluff-er? Have you an am-bi-tion to be a per-form-er? To be a per-form-er, get read-y to suf-fer a chron-ic con-di-tion the rest of your life. _____ If

bat - ic, op - er - at - ic? _____ Be ec - stat - ic, _____ Here you
(optional:) (You'll go

are, _____ You can be the sec - ond un - der - stud - y to the
far,) _____ (might)

star! So

Tempo I

N.C.

join the pro - fes - sion! The price of ad - mis - sion is just an ob - ses - sion to be a per - form - er, to

DIMPLES

Music by CY COLEMAN
Lyrics by CAROLYN LEIGH

Oh! dem dog-gone dim-ples! Oh! dey did it a-gain!

Tell me why a lit-tle in-den-ta-tion should start a crim-i-nal in-ves-ti-ga-tion!

Oh! dem dog-gone dim-ples!

If I ev-er go to da pen,
If I get in trou-ble with men,

DON'T ASK THE LADY
WHAT THE LADY DID BEFORE

Music by CY COLEMAN
Lyrics by CAROLYN LEIGH

D.S. al Coda

if the __ la - dy's been a - broad!

CODA

ask what the la - dy's do - in'

don't ask how well she's do - in' what oth - er swell she's do - in'
(Now)

ask what the hell she's do - in' now.

HERE'S TO US

Music by CY COLEMAN
Lyrics by CAROLYN LEIGH

Freely

Now what shall we raise a toast to? The
cares we once were host to, the banks we owed the most to have van-ished and three
cheers! There's no-bod-y left to toast to, ex-cept the ones we're
close to. It may not be Em-'ly Post to say it, but, here's how! And I must say it:

Moderately bright bounce

Here's to us, my dar-ling, my dear, ____ here's to us to - night; _____ Not for what might hap - pen next year, ____ for it might not be near - ly as bright _____

But here's to us, for bet - ter or worse, ____ and for
And here's to us, for all that we have ____ and the

I WANNA BE YOURS

Music by CY COLEMAN
Lyrics by CAROLYN LEIGH

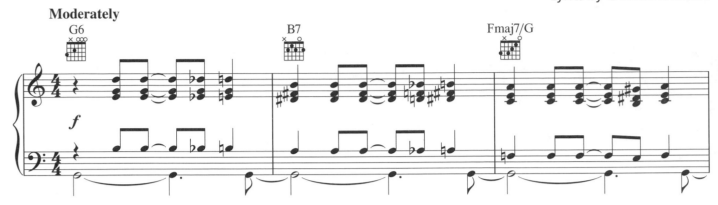

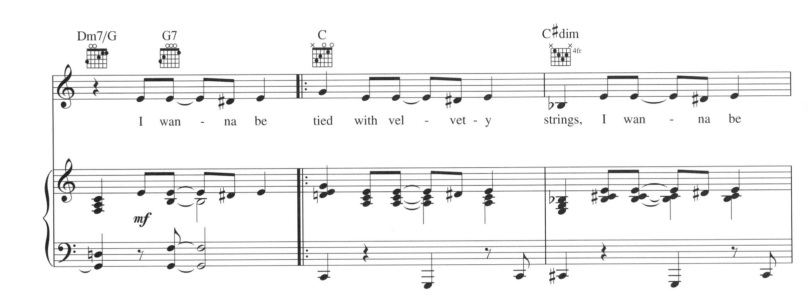

I wan - na be tied with vel - vet - y strings, I wan - na be

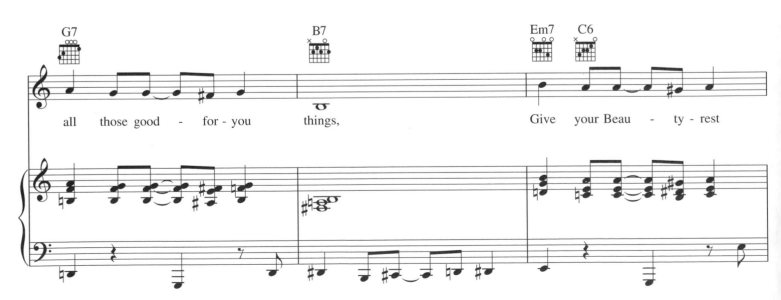

all those good - for - you things,   Give your Beau - ty - rest

I'VE GOT YOUR NUMBER

Music by CY COLEMAN
Lyrics by CAROLYN LEIGH

Moderate, with a relaxed swinging beat

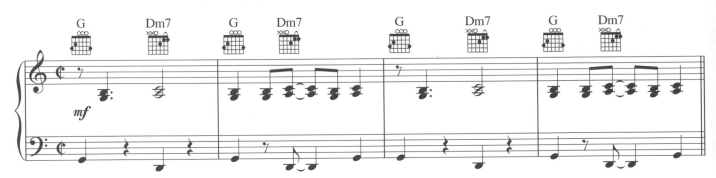

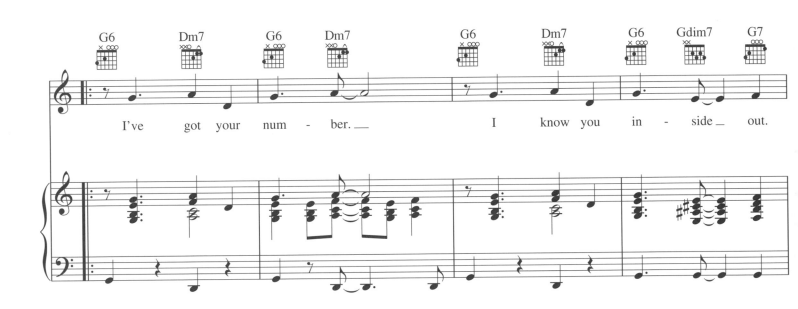

I've got your num - ber. ___ I know you in - side ___ out.

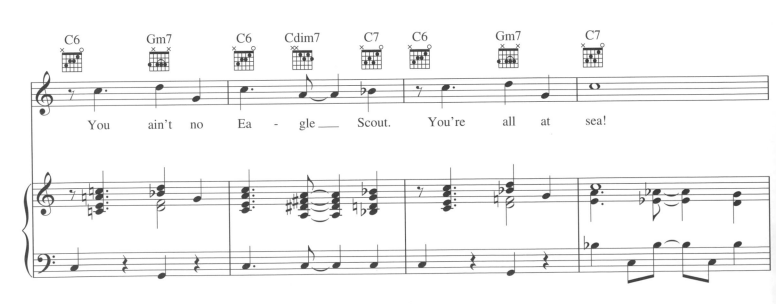

You ain't no Ea - gle ___ Scout. You're all at sea!

LE GRAND BOOM BOOM

Music by CY COLEMAN
Lyrics by CAROLYN LEIGH

Moderately bright

rette!" _____ And clear his throat, _____ "Lest you for - get!" _____ And here I
rot?" _____ He'll start to snore, _____ the rest you know, _____ she'll say once

quote: If ze girl, boom boom and ze boy, boom
man, boom boom and ze wife, boom
more: If ze girl, boom boom and ze boy, boom

boom and zey get to - gez - zer and zey both boom
boom 'though it's just a le - gal - ized for life boom
boom and zey get to - gez - zer and zey both boom

boom,
boom, c'est le grand boom boom, et le grand boom boom, zat's ze
boom,

LITTLE ME

Music by CY COLEMAN
Lyrics by CAROLYN LEIGH

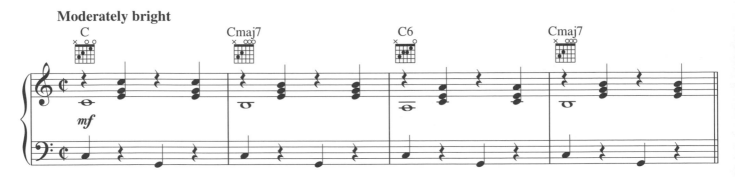

ON THE OTHER SIDE OF THE TRACKS

Music by CY COLEMAN
Lyrics by CAROLYN LEIGH

POOR LITTLE HOLLYWOOD STAR

Music by CY COLEMAN
Lyrics by CAROLYN LEIGH

Once you were an or-di-nar-y, av-'rage lit-tle girl from Il-li-nois, _____

Once it was an or-di-nar-y, av-'rage lit-tle life and what a

joy! _____ Sud-den suc-cess caught you, I guess,

REAL LIVE GIRL

Music by CY COLEMAN
Lyrics by CAROLYN LEIGH

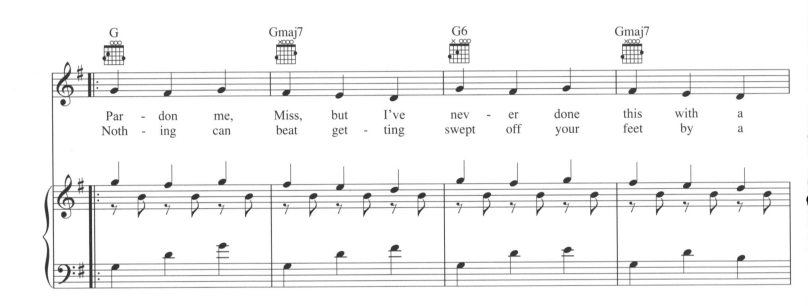

Par - don me, Miss, but I've nev - er done this with a
Noth - ing can beat get - ting swept off your feet by a

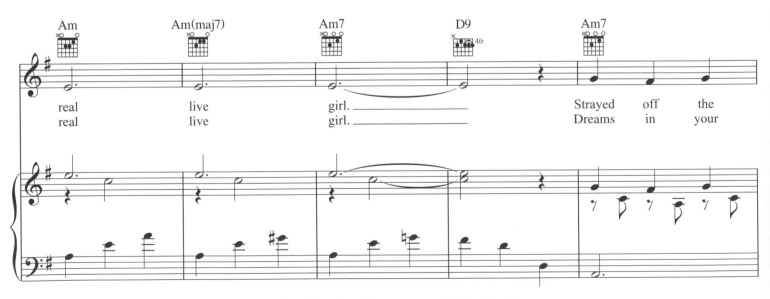

real live girl. _____ Strayed off the
real live girl. _____ Dreams in your